Making a Great Exhibition

Doro Globus and Rose Blake

David Zwirner Books

For Tristan

How is a GREAT
exhibition made?
It takes many people
with lots of different
skills. Let's take a look!

This is Viola. She is a sculptor. She makes art out of rock, marble, metal, and clay. Some things she makes are even bigger than you.

This is Sebastian. He is a painter. He makes colorful pictures out of shapes and lines on canvases of all sizes. They are both artists.

Both of these artworks are abstract: they are made out of shapes and forms but don't look like something from real life.

This is what one of Viola's sculptures looks like when she's done.

This is one of Sebastian's paintings.

Artists work in studios that can come in all shapes and sizes. Viola lives in a big city and uses an old toy factory for her studio.

Sebastian lives in the countryside and his studio is part of his house.

This is the inside of Viola's big studio. She has lots of assistants helping to make her sculptures. It is a busy place and everyone must be very careful.

Schedule

STUDIO
SCHEDULE

THE EXHIBITION!

T-256

Painting

Blow torch

Polishing

Ladder

Rock

Powerpack

Studies

Chair

Canvas

Phone

This is Sebastian's painting studio. He works by himself, although sometimes his cat gets involved! His studio is full of paint pots and brushes. He makes his paintings as big as the wall will allow.

EXHIBITION COUNTDOWN!

Schedule

Speaker

Paint pots

Assistant

Artists use things they like to give them ideas about what to make. Viola likes dinosaurs, shells, ancient art, masks, and cookies.

Flute

Fossils

Mars

Cycladic figures

Writings by other artists

HOUSE HITS

Snails

Brutalist buildings

Sebastian likes candy, flowers, Egypt, animals, and quilts.

Squash

Licorice allsorts

BACH
MASS in B MINOR

Bird of Paradise

Greek vases

American quilts

Chocolate milk

RUMI
SELECTED POEMS

apartamento

Sneakers

Lined paper

A snail catches Viola's eye.

Being an artist means seeing the everyday world a bit differently. Viola sees shapes everywhere she goes.

She waits for a big piece of stone to be delivered from a quarry.

She uses a chisel to form her sculpture.

She sketches the snail with a pencil, slowly breaking it apart.

She finds forms like circles, swirls, and lines in nature and makes them into something brand new.

Her assistant smooths out the rough edges.

Sebastian is inspired on a walk.

He makes sketches on the computer.

Sebastian also has a special way of looking at the world around him. He likes to examine the way colors meet each other. He does quick sketches wherever he goes, but when he gets back to his studio he breaks down what he saw into small parts, creating new forms.

He paints details on small canvases.

He picks his favorite study and enlarges it.

Here are Sara and Tom. They are art handlers.
It is their job to pack up all the artworks
carefully so they don't break on their way
to the museum. They use big wooden crates,
lots of soft foam, and metal bands. They are
getting Viola's sculptures and Sebastian's
paintings ready to ship to the museum.

FRAGILE

Cloud

Airplane

Whale

Palm Tree

The artworks travel up to
10,000 miles from the studios:

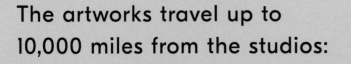

5,545 miles by cargo jet,
9,938 miles by container ship,
or 320 miles by truck.

HMS TRISTAN

Ship

MUSEUM

Truck

At last, after a long journey and many weeks of travel,
the sculptures and paintings arrive at the museum.
Everyone is so excited to get started on this great exhibition!

This is Cliff. He is a curator. It is his job to pick what goes inside the museum and where each artwork should be placed. Cliff is getting ready for Viola and Sebastian's exhibition.

He has made a model with miniature versions of all the artworks so he can decide where each one should go. It is just like a dollhouse.

It takes many people to make a great exhibition.

Museum director
"I'm in charge of the
whole museum."

Art handler
"You can find me at work
installing the exhibition."

Registrar
"I keep track of the works
through their journey."

Events assistant
"I make sure all of the
dinners and parties are fun."

Archivist
"I keep everything from
the exhibition for people
to look at in the future."

Development director
"I help the museum raise money to put on the exhibition."

Conservator
"I carefully fix anything that may have gotten damaged."

Communications manager
"I make sure the whole world knows about the exhibition."

Museum guard
"I protect the artworks and answer lots of questions."

Educator
"I come up with fun activities to teach people all about art."

Light

Ruler

Level

Here are art handlers Isabel and Liam. It is their job to hang the paintings on the wall and place the sculptures. They must be very, very careful.

They are working alongside Sam, who is a lighting designer. It is Sam's job to get the lights just right so everyone can see all the details in the artworks.

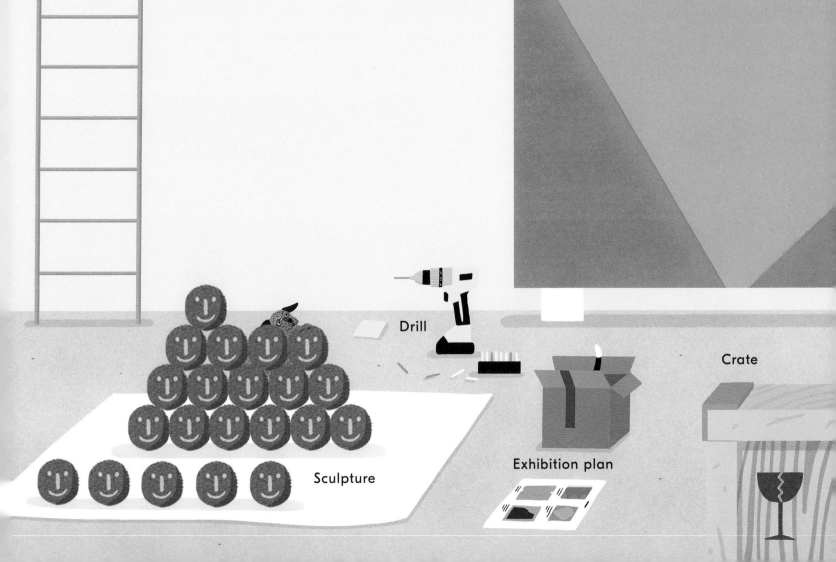

Drill

Crate

Sculpture

Exhibition plan

Visiting the graphic designers who put the pieces of the book together.

This is Dorothy. She is the editor who works on books about artists and their exhibitions.

Making sure that the writing doesn't have any mistakes.

Checking that the colors will look like the real artworks.

Watching the book print on a very, very big machine.

The book arrives just in time for the opening.

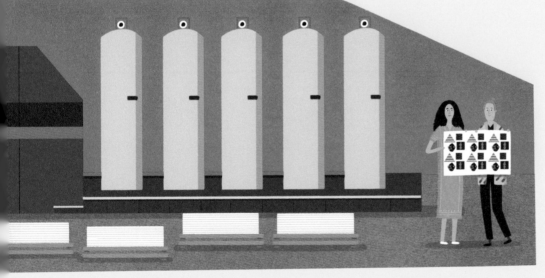

Books are often made about an exhibition so that visitors can bring the art home with them. Lots of different people come together to make them.

Cliff practices his
welcome speech.

After the paintings are hung and the sculptures are put in the right place, Viola and Sebastian meet curator Cliff to take a look. There are still a lot of finishing touches to take care of.

The artists get their portrait taken.

Wall labels are placed below the paintings.

Opening night is a time to celebrate! It is the first time the exhibition is open to family and friends. After a tour of the museum, the artists and everyone who worked on the exhibition enjoy a fun and very special dinner.

A toast is made to thank
the artists and the team.

Cheers!

Bread

Cheese

Prawns

Radishes

People young and old come to see the artworks. They think about how they were made, what inspired them, and what they are looking at. It also takes you, the visitor, to make a great exhibition.

And what a GREAT
exhibition it is!

Making a Great Exhibition
by Doro Globus and Rose Blake

Published by
David Zwirner Books
529 West 20th Street, 2nd Floor
New York, New York 10011
+1 212 727 2070
davidzwirnerbooks.com

Design: A Practice for Everyday Life, London
Copy Editor: Elizabeth Gordon
Production Manager: Jules Thomson
Color Separations: VeronaLibri, Verona
Printing: VeronaLibri, Verona

Typefaces: Alwa Display and GT Eesti Display
Paper: Magno Natural, 170gsm

First published 2021. Second printing 2022.

Distributed in the United States and Canada by
Simon & Schuster, Inc.
1230 Avenue of the Americas
New York, New York 10020
simonandschuster.com

Distributed outside the United States and Canada by
Thames & Hudson, Ltd.
181A High Holborn
London WC1V 7QX
thamesandhudson.com

ISBN 978-1-64423-049-7
Library of Congress Control Number: 2021907645

Printed in Italy

This book would not have been possible without
the urging of Tristan, who asked every day for a
kids' book to be made for him. Being raised in the
art world, the daughters of an artist and a curator,
we must thank our parents for always encouraging
creativity. Thank you to David Zwirner and Lucas
Zwirner for encouraging our vision to share the arts
with children. Thank you to Roger Thorp for his
advice. Thank you to the great group of women who
brought it all together: Kirsty Carter, Joanna Rutter,
and Emma Thomas at A Practice for Everyday Life,
Jules Thomson, Claire Bidwell, and the team at
VeronaLibri for the gorgeous production, Anne Wehr,
Elizabeth Gordon, Molly Stein, Susan Cernek,
Sara Chan, Erin Pinover, Julia Lukacher, Susi Kenna,
Nicola von Velsen, Giovanna Ballin, Sophie Giraud,
Britta Nelson, Kelly Reynolds, and Andrea Burnett for
their eagle eyes and support, and to all our friends,
family, and colleagues who tested it out for us.